HEALTH MATTERS

Attention Deficit Disorder

Carol Baldwin

Heinemann Library
Chicago, Illinois

©2003 Reed Educational & Professional Publishing
Published by Heinemann Library,
an imprint of Reed Educational & Professional
Publishing, Chicago, Illinois

Customer Service 888-454-2279

Visit our website at www.heinemannlibrary.com

Designed by Patricia Stevenson
Printed and bound in the United States
by Lake Book Manufacturing

07 06 05 04 03
10 9 8 7 6 5 4 3 2 1

Library of Congress Cataloging-in-Publication Data
Baldwin, Carol, 1943–
   Attention deficit disorder / Carol Baldwin.
      p. cm. — (Health matters)
Includes bibliographical references and index.
   ISBN 1-40340-249-3
   1. Attention-deficit hyperactivity disorder—
   Juvenile literature. [1. Attention-deficit
   hyperactivity disorder.] I. Title.

RJ506.H9 B345 2002
618.92'8589—dc21
                              2001007971

Acknowledgments
The author and publishers are grateful to the
following for permission to reproduce copyright
material:

Cover photograph by MMI/Stock Boston, Inc.

p.4 Jerrican Gaillard/Science Photo Library; p. 5
Bob Daemmrich/Stock Boston, Inc.; p. 6 David
Woodroffe; p. 7 Garry Watson/Science Photo
Library; p. 8 Ariel Skelley/Corbis Stock Market; pp.
9, 18,19 Trevor Clifford/Heinemann Library; p. 10
MMI/Stock Boston, Inc.; p. 11 Dorit
Lombroso/Index Stock Imagery/PictureQuest; p. 12
Michael Newman/PhotoEdit/PictureQuest; p. 13
Ann McCarthy/Corbis Stock Market; pp. 14, 22 Bob
Daemmrich/Stock Boston, Inc./PictureQuest; p. 15
Myrleen Ferguson Cate/PhotoEdit; pp. 16, 25 David
Young-Wolff/PhotoEdit/PictureQuest; p. 17 K.
Beebe/Custom Medical Stock Photo, Inc.; p. 20
Ulrike Welsch/Photo Researchers, Inc.; p. 21 Anne
Griffiths Belt/Corbis; p. 23 Jonathan
Nourok/PhotoEdit; p. 24 David Stover/Stock
South/PictureQuest; p. 26 Richard Nowitz/Photo
Researchers, Inc.; p. 27 Mitchell Gerber/Corbis; p.
28L Colin Mulvaney; p. 28R Mark Lennihan/AP
Wide World Photos

Every effort has been made to contact copyright
holders of any material reproduced in this book.
Any omissions will be rectified in subsequent
printings if notice is given to the publisher.

Some words are shown in bold, **like this.** You can find out what they
mean by looking in the glossary.

Contents

What Is Attention Deficit Disorder?

Attention deficit disorder (ADD) is a **condition** that causes people to have problems learning, behaving, and getting along with others. People with ADD may have one or more of these three **symptoms:**

◆ **Inattention:** People who are inattentive find it hard to think about one thing at a time. They usually have trouble paying attention to any one thing for very long.

◆ **Hyperactivity:** People who are hyperactive have trouble sitting still. They might also have problems being quiet.

◆ **Impulsiveness:** People who are impulsive don't think before they say or do things. They can say and do things without first thinking about how other people might feel or what might happen as a result of their actions.

This may sound like a lot, but having attention deficit disorder does not make a person very different from anyone else. Everybody is a little different in his or her own way. Most people who have ADD are nice, friendly people. They make good friends because they are full of energy and interested in doing many different things.

At school, children have to learn to pay attention, raise their hands, sit still, wait their turn, and do their work. Children who have ADD may find some or all of these things very difficult.

Types of ADD

Not all people who have ADD have the same kind of difficulties. There are three different types of attention deficit disorders.

Inattentive: Some people with ADD only have trouble paying attention. They have a hard time thinking about just one thing or keeping their minds on the most important thing. This is called being distracted. They tend to forget what they were supposed to be doing. They also tend to be shy and quiet.

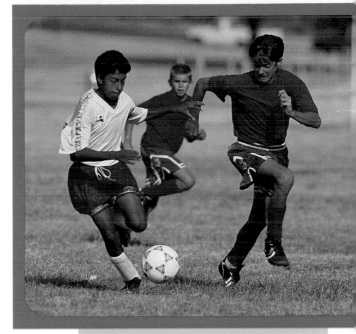

Many children who have ADHD feel the need to be moving all the time. Active games are one way to use some of that extra energy.

Hyperactive/Impulsive: Other people who have ADD have trouble with hyperactivity and impulsiveness. They seem to have extra energy and like to keep moving all the time. They often get bored easily. They may also lose their patience quickly and lose their tempers easily. This type of ADD is called attention deficit hyperactivity disorder, or ADHD.

Combined: Still other people have problems with inattention, hyperactivity, and impulsiveness. These people are also said to have ADHD and they usually have the most difficulty in school and at home.

What Causes ADD?

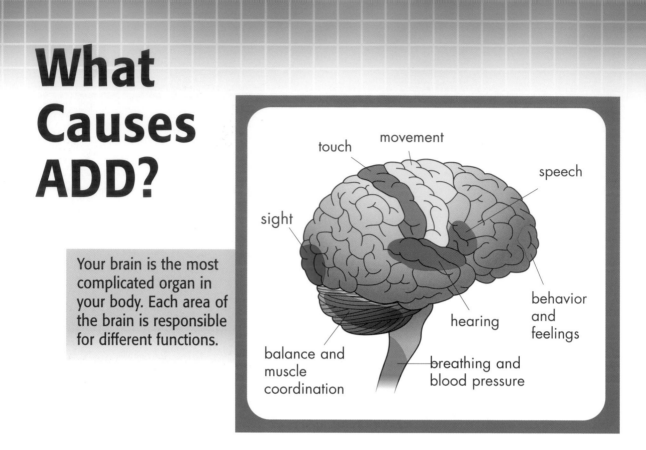

Your brain is the most complicated organ in your body. Each area of the brain is responsible for different functions.

touch

movement

speech

sight

behavior and feelings

hearing

balance and muscle coordination

breathing and blood pressure

Many people think attention deficit disorder is a new **condition.** But the reason people hear more about it today is that doctors have become better at recognizing its **symptoms** and understanding the causes. They now think that ADD is caused by small differences in the way certain people's brains work.

The brain's job

Your brain controls your whole body. It also controls how you think, learn, and feel. Messages from your brain travel to different parts of your body and tell them what to do in different situations. Different parts of your brain have different jobs. Some parts of your brain respond to signals from your **sensory organs** so you can see, hear, taste, touch, and smell. Other parts of your brain allow you to move and keep your balance. Still other parts of your brain help you learn, remember, make decisions, and control your feelings.

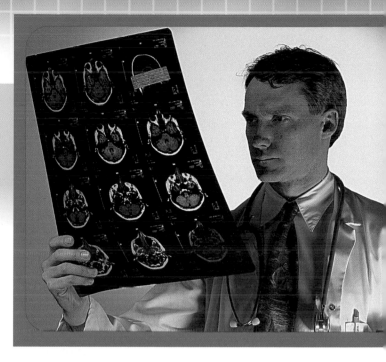

Scientists may soon be able to explain exactly what causes ADD and find new ways of helping people who have it.

Chemicals and the brain

Your brain is made up of billions of tiny **nerve** cells. These cells connect to each other to sort out the information that is sent to your brain. The way these nerves connect lets you think and make decisions. For example, suppose you start to cross a street. Your eyes send a message to the nerves in your brain that a car is coming. Your brain then sends a message, through nerves, to your muscles to step back onto the sidewalk.

Nerve cells rely on **chemicals** to be able to do their jobs. The chemicals are made in different parts of your brain in tiny, but very exact, amounts. They affect the way messages are sent between nerve cells. A person who has ADD might have too little of a chemical in some parts of their brain. This affects how their brain controls their behavior. A friend with ADD may behave differently from your other friends because of these tiny chemical differences. But ADD is not an illness or a disease. People with ADD are just as healthy as anyone else.

Other factors

Doctors know that ADD shows up more often in some families than in others. Having ADD can run in families, much like having red hair or brown eyes. People with ADD might be **predisposed** to having lower levels of certain brain **chemicals.**

Doctors also think ADD might be caused by problems that a child's mother had before or during the child's birth. Some of these include the mother smoking, drinking alcohol, or having a blood infection while she was pregnant.

Other factors that doctors are studying as possible causes of ADD are chemicals in the **environment.** Breathing in or swallowing dust that contains **lead** can affect how a child's brain works. This can cause children to be **impulsive** or **hyperactive,** and have difficulty learning. Some doctors also think that chemicals sprayed on fruits and vegetables might cause ADD.

A different view of ADD

Some doctors don't think of attention deficit disorder as a **condition** that causes problem behaviors. Instead, they think of the behavior patterns of ADD as good qualities rather than problems. The chart below shows differences in the way these behaviors can be viewed.

Behaviors viewed as problems	Behaviors viewed as good qualities
Can't pay attention to anything for very long	Always aware of everything that's going on
Acts without thinking about the results	Willing and able to take risks
Not organized; impulsive	Ready to change quickly if something doesn't work out
Daydreams	Enjoys thinking about new and interesting things
Has difficulty following directions	Is independent; likes to do things his or her own way

Differences in the brains of children who have ADD make it hard for them to pay attention to things. However, something new and different, like a new computer game, will usually keep their attention.

Diagnosing ADD

Common signs

Children with ADD have problems following rules and instructions. They don't mean to break the rules or to not follow instructions, something else just distracts them.

The ways that a child's ADD affects their behavior from one day to the next can be very different. For example, a child might get a perfect score on a science quiz one day and fail another science quiz two days later. At home, a child might do his homework one day, but forget to bring his school books home the next. Or he may do his homework and forget to take it school. These children's teachers and parents are never sure what to expect from one day to the next.

In school, classmates who are **hyperactive** can be easy to recognize. They are always on the move, and find it hard to sit still for very long. They may also act out and have a hard time following a teacher's instructions to settle down.

Children who have problems with **inattention** often appear to be tired or confused in school. They might seem to spend a lot of time daydreaming.

Some mothers of young children who have ADHD describe them as being in constant motion, breaking toys and disturbing everything in their paths.

Finding out

Sometimes parents spot the signs of ADD, especially hyperactivity, when their children are toddlers. They wonder why their child can't sit still long enough to finish a simple puzzle. They question why their child runs around out of control at home, on playgrounds, or at other people's homes.

Young children with ADHD are always on the go, climbing onto and getting into things. Parents feel like they can't turn their backs on these children for a minute. If they do, the child could be turning over the trash can or running out the door and down the street.

However, teachers are sometimes the first to notice that something is wrong. They see many children every day, so they can tell when a student is behaving or learning differently from other children of the same age. In a classroom, a child who can't sit still or pay attention like the other children is easy for a teacher to spot.

Treating ADD

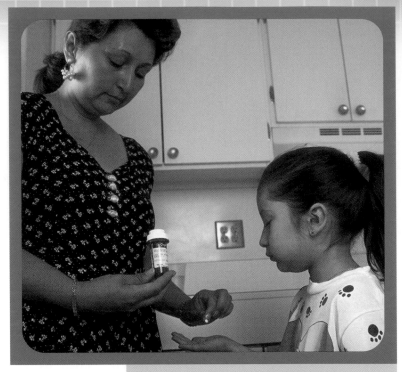

Some people find that medicine helps them learn ways of dealing with their **condition** so that eventually they need less medicine, or maybe none at all.

Think about how you feel when you haven't had enough sleep and are really tired. Maybe you find it hard to concentrate on your schoolwork. You find your mind wandering off. Maybe you're in a bad mood and lose your temper. Then you get a good night's sleep and those feelings go away. For some of your friends with ADD, this is how it feels after they take medicine to help their **symptoms.** They find they are able to concentrate in class and don't daydream as much. They also don't get angry as easily.

Not all children with ADD take medicine, but some of your classmates probably find that it helps them. There are a number of different medicines for treating ADD. The most common one is called **Ritalin.** Children usually take a small number of Ritalin pills every day. Sometimes children with ADD need to take their medicine more than once a day, so you might notice them visiting the school nurse at lunchtime for a pill.

How medicine helps

Ritalin and other medicines used to treat attention deficit disorders are **stimulants.** They work by increasing the action of certain **chemicals** in the part of the brain that controls behavior.

In a way, medicine acts like the brakes on a racecar, allowing people with ADD to slow down. Medicine allows children with ADD to better control their behavior. It also helps them concentrate on what they are doing, both at home and in school.

Most children who take medicine for their ADD are less **impulsive** and have fewer problems getting along with their classmates. But some children may not be helped by medicine. So, even if a child's doctor **prescribes** medicine, it should never be the only treatment that a child has.

Some children find that taking medicine for ADD helps them at home and at school. They feel happier because they know they can do more things without trouble.

Doing without medicine

Some people may not take medicine to treat their **condition.** Some parents and children don't like the idea of taking medicine for ADD. They might not like the **side effects** that the medicines can have. Or the child might be among the group of people who finds that medicine doesn't help them. They might even feel worse when they take medicine.

Some doctors say that side effects can be handled by taking less medicine. Even so, some people still want to deal with their ADD without the help of any medicines. It's important to remember that children should use the kind of help that works best for them.

Natural remedies

Today many people like to take what are called "natural remedies." These are substances from plants or other natural sources that are meant to improve illnesses and **conditions.** Some people find that taking vitamins or **herbs** can help their ADD. It's often hard to prove whether these natural remedies help, but many people believe they do.

Large doses of vitamins and herbs may have side effects just as other medicines do.

Specialists and counselors may suggest that a child with ADD keep a behavior diary. This can help the child prevent future problems.

What other treatments can help?

Some children with ADD may talk to a special teacher or a school counselor. Some may also see a **specialist** to help them change their behavior. These people talk with the child's family members too, so everyone can work together. This is called **family counseling**.

Some children with ADD may keep a diary to write down any behavior problems they have right after they happen. Many children understand what went wrong only after something has happened. The hard part is keeping it from happening again. With a diary, they can look back to see what caused the problem. Then they can think of ways to change things. They can keep a behavior diary alone or with the help of a teacher or a parent.

Classmates with ADD

All children are different and all children who have ADD have different kinds of problems. What does it really mean to be **inattentive, hyperactive,** or **impulsive?** Some of the signs of ADD that you might see in classmates are described here.

Inattention in school

Classmates who are inattentive don't really misbehave in school. They're usually shy and don't volunteer to answer questions. If the teacher calls on them in class, they might not even know what question the teacher asked. They usually try very hard to concentrate on schoolwork, but sometimes their minds just drift away. They might start working on a class assignment but then notice a bird outside the window and forget what they're supposed to be doing. They might forget to copy down a homework assignment. They have trouble following a teacher's instructions and may seem to be confused a lot of the time. They often get distracted by other things even when they're talking to people.

Some people say that having an attention deficit disorder is a little overwhelming. It's not that they can't pay attention to anything—it's that they pay attention to everything.

Many students with ADHD get bored if they have to sit still for very long. They feel better if they can stand up or move around from time to time.

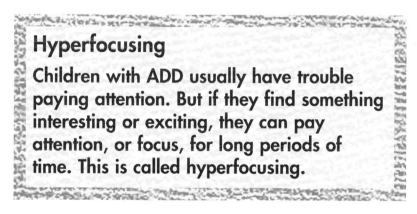

Hyperfocusing

Children with ADD usually have trouble paying attention. But if they find something interesting or exciting, they can pay attention, or focus, for long periods of time. This is called hyperfocusing.

Hyperactivity in school

Do you have a classmate who always seems kind of hyperactive? Hyperactive children are full of energy. They can't seem to sit still. They squirm around in their seats. They tap their fingers or pencils on the desk. They're always trying to find an excuse to get out of their seats and move around. They may do poorly on a test or an assignment because they rush through it. Their work is often sloppy and hard to read. They often try to do several things at once, and they might move on to a new project before they have finished the last one. It's very hard for these children to slow down when their minds and bodies are so active.

Impulsiveness in school

Many children with ADD are very **impulsive.** Instead of thinking before they act, they act before they think. They might answer questions in class without raising their hands. Sometimes they might not even let the teacher finish asking the question. They might interrupt you when you are talking to someone else. They might even interrupt the teacher in class. They often lose things, and their desks and lockers can look like disaster areas.

They might say the first thing that pops into their heads because they don't realize that doing this could hurt someone's feelings. They may push or hit someone at recess when they are upset because they find it hard to control how they act.

Sometimes they do dangerous things like running into the street after a ball or pushing a child off a swing. They aren't trying to be mean. Later, after they have thought about it, they feel bad about the things that they did.

Children with ADHD may find it harder than others to control their behavior. They may do things that annoy other people, like cutting in line.

Ways of learning

Everyone learns in different ways. For example, some people remember things better if they write them down. Others are happier to have things explained out loud to them. Students with ADD often find it hard to learn. They are just as smart as other children, it's just that they may learn things in different ways.

Having a little extra time to finish a test can give students who have ADD a fairer chance to show what they have learned.

Some ways people learn best

- touching, moving, and handling objects

- looking at photos, drawings, and videos

- using numbers and reasoning things out

- reading and understanding written words

- listening to spoken words and to tones and rhythms

Classmates who have ADD may take longer to finish assignments than your other classmates. You might notice that the teacher lets them have more time to finish a test. For them, this can mean the difference between passing or failing the test.

How You Can Help

If you have a friend who has ADD, you can do some things to help him or her. For example, if you're playing a game, remind him or her of the game's rules because he or she might have trouble remembering them. And if your friend wants to do something that could be dangerous, like climbing to the top of a big tree, remind him or her that they might get hurt.

Just being understanding can help, too. Some children who have ADD say it makes them feel different from other children in their class. They might also feel like there is something wrong with them. Talking with your friend about this can help them feel better.

Finally, when your friend does something well, like making a really good poster in class, tell him or her how good it is. Everyone likes to be told they're good at something.

When you work on a school project with a friend who has ADD, you can help your friend keep on task by reminding him or her from time to time what the two of you are supposed to be doing.

Ideas that work

You can help your friend get his or her schoolwork done by focusing on your own work and not goofing around in class. Students with ADD sometimes need help from their classmates to stay on task.

Students with ADD often need to take extra steps to stay focused on their work.

Here are some other ways that children who have ADD stay focused. Some of these may help you, too:

- sitting away from distractions, such as windows and doors
- sitting close to the teacher and the chalkboard
- sitting near classmates who do their work and don't talk as much
- asking teachers to repeat tasks or write them down
- using a homework notebook and writing down every assignment right away
- keeping their desks clear of everything but the books or papers they are working on
- breaking tasks down into smaller parts so they can concentrate on one thing at a time
- before leaving school, running through a checklist to make sure they have everything they need to get their homework done

Visiting a Friend with ADD

For a friend with ADD, life can be a little out of control at times. A home life filled with routine and order can help them. That might mean waking up, eating meals, doing homework, and going to bed at the same time every day. But that's not always as simple as it sounds.

Your friend might have trouble getting ready for school in the morning. He or she might get up from the breakfast table so often that there's not enough time to finish eating. These behaviors can make everybody else in the family late, too. It's not good to let a person get away with this behavior just because he or she has ADD. Most children just need help learning to do things differently. Your friend might find that a reward, such as extra time to watch television, is enough to help them concentrate on getting ready for school on time.

Children with ADD often have to hurry to make it to school in the morning. If you walk to school with a friend who has ADD, he may not be ready on time.

Having a brother or sister with ADD can be difficult. But once they've been working with doctors and **specialists** to improve their behavior, their brothers and sisters usually find that they enjoy spending more time with them.

Getting along

If you visit a friend who has ADD, don't be surprised if they don't get along with a brother or sister. Of course, if you have brothers and sisters, you might not always get along either. However, children with ADD take up a lot of their parents' time. This can sometimes cause problems for other children in the family. Brothers and sisters sometimes find it hard to live with a child who is always causing problems. They may get upset because their parents pay so much attention to the child with ADD.

However, when the family has rules, rewards, and punishments for a child with ADD, things usually improve. For example, one rule might be that your friend can't just walk into a brother or sister's room without knocking or asking first. If your friend breaks the rule, a punishment might be no television for a day. If he or she follows a rule for an entire week, however, then the whole family might go out for ice cream.

Dealing with homework

For students who have ADD and their parents, homework can be a real problem. Children who are **inattentive** may forget to take their books and papers home. Or they might have such a hard time concentrating on their work that they never seem to be able to finish it. Children who are **impulsive** may make mistakes on their homework because they answer questions without thinking them through. Their writing may also be hard to read because they hurry so much. And children who are **hyperactive** might have difficulty sitting still long enough to get their work done.

Working together

If you go to a friend's house after school to work on a homework project, there are some ways you can help. You can make sure you both have everything you need before you leave school. You can also work with your friend to break the project down into small parts. Then it's easier for both of you to concentrate on one part of the project at time.

Many children with ADD have messy handwriting. If you and a friend are working together on an assignment, using a computer will solve that problem.

Many children who are hyperactive find good ways to use their extra energy. This boy is a volunteer at the local animal shelter. Twice a week after school, he walks dogs. He also plays with the animals and brushes their coats.

Spending time together

A friend who has ADHD might have a lot of extra energy. What are some of the things the two of you can do together? First, you have to think "active." Sports are a great way to use energy and stay healthy. You and your friend might join a softball, baseball, swimming, or soccer team together.

You both could get some good exercise by walking your dog or a neighbor's dog. Or you might have fun building a fort or an obstacle course together. Just make sure that the activities you choose to do together are safe. Your friend might need you to remind him not to do something dangerous.

If your friend likes video games, you might find you don't need to be as active. Your friend will probably be able to really concentrate on the game, and you may have a hard time beating him or her.

Summer camps allow children with ADHD to use their extra energy in positive ways.

Summer camp

Many children look forward to attending summer camp. The activities of summer camp, such as swimming, boating, soccer, and basketball, are great for children with lots of energy and especially those with ADD. Camps that offer arts and crafts, music, dance, and drama allow campers to express their creativity. Many camps also have computer centers and science labs. Campers might learn to build and launch rockets, make a weather station, or even build a radio. Going to camp with a friend who has ADD could turn out to be a great experience for both of you.

Some children who have ADD might choose to go to a special camp with other children who have the same **condition.** If they have difficulty controlling their **symptoms,** a camp with special programs allows them to enjoy all of the activities of a summer camp while learning ways to control their behavior and be successful in school and at home.

ADD Success Stories

People with ADD grow up to be happy, successful adults. You might want to share the stories of these people with someone you know who has ADD.

In spite of having attention deficit disorder and **dyslexia,** Woody Harrelson was awarded a scholarship to Hanover College in Indiana. There he earned a degree in English and theatrical arts. After college, he went to New York to start his acting career. Later, he moved to Los Angeles where he acted in television and movies. In 1996, he was nominated for an Academy Award. He is also interested in the environment and owns a small piece of rainforest in Central America.

Famous people who may have had ADD

Many experts think that a lot of famous people had ADD because of what has been written about their behavior. For example, Leonardo da Vinci was famous for his paintings, but he only managed to do seventeen paintings in 67 years, and some of those were never finished. Nikola Tesla was an inventor who started work on many different inventions, but rarely finished them. Albert Einstein and Thomas Edison also showed signs of having ADD.

Stephanie Brush has always had problems with **inattention,** but not **hyperactivity.** Medicine used to treat her ADD did not help her. She has said she probably tries ten times harder than other people to do a good job on a project, and takes much longer to finish things. But she has learned to cope well with her challenges—in addition to being a writer and songwriter, she also works as an actress and singer.

Dan O'Brien went to the University of Idaho on a track scholarship, but had problems and dropped out. Then his coach at college realized that Dan might have ADHD. After seeing a doctor, Dan was put on medication for his condition. The medicine helped him focus. Although he later had to stop taking the medicine because of **side effects,** by then he understood why he had trouble concentrating. Instead of medicine, Dan uses deep-breathing exercises to help him concentrate and focus. He has learned to set goals and focus on them. The result was a gold medal in the decathlon at the 1996 Olympics.

Learning More about ADD

If you have friends with ADD, accept them and like them for being themselves. Remember, ADD isn't something a person should be ashamed or embarrassed about. If you want to learn more about ADD, there are several groups that have information about attention deficit disorders. Going through this information with parents and teachers can help you better understand the causes, treatments, and **symptoms** of ADD.

Children with Attention Deficit Disorder (Ch.A.D.D.)
499 Northwest 70th Avenue, Suite 308
Plantation, FL 33317
305-587-3700

Attention Deficit Disorder Association (ADDA)
2620 Ivy Place
Toledo, OH 43613
419-472-1286

Both of these groups also have websites with information just for kids. There are also other websites where you can find more information about ADD.

Glossary

chemical substance that produces a change in another substance. Some chemicals in the brain help transmit messages from one nerve cell to another. Some chemicals in the environment can cause or make ADD symptoms worse.

condition health problem that a person has for a long time, perhaps for all of his or her life

diagnose to recognize what illness or condition a person has

dyslexia condition that makes it hard for a person to read, write, and spell

environment surroundings; everything around a person, including people, plants, animals, water, air, buildings, and towns

family counseling when family members talk with a doctor or counselor to solve problems that one or more family members are having

herb plant that can be used in cooking or for making medicine

hyperactive, hyperactivity not able to stay still

impulsive, impulsiveness doing or saying things without first thinking about them

inattentive, inattention finding it hard to pay attention to anything for very long

lead soft metal that is toxic to people

nerve tiny bundle of cells that passes information between different parts of the brain or between the brain and other body parts

predisposed ability or likelihood of something happening. Some children are predisposed to having low levels of certain brain chemicals.

prescribe to tell someone the kind and amount of medicine to take

Ritalin name of one kind of medicine that is used to treat attention deficit disorders. Such medicines do not cure people, but may help ease the symptoms.

sensory organ body part, such as the eyes, ears, nose, tongue, and skin, that gathers information from surroundings

side effect unwanted effect of a medicine

specialist person who studies and works in a specific area of knowledge

stimulant something, like a medicine or a drug, that makes a part of the body more active for a while

symptom change in the body that is a sign of a health problem; the effects an illness or a condition has on the body

More Books to Read

Beal, Eileen. *Everything You Need to Know about ADD/ADHD.* New York: Rosen Publishing Group, 1998.

Dwyer, Kathleen. *What Do You Mean I Have Attention Deficit Disorder?* New York: Walker & Company, 1996.

Ingersoll, Barbara. *Distant Drums, Different Drummers: A Guide for Young People with ADHD.* Bethesda, Md.: Cape Publications, 1995.

Moragne, Wendy. *Attention Deficit Disorder.* Brookfield, Conn.: Millbrook Press, 1996.

Silverstein, Alvin, Virginia Silverstein, and Laura Silverstein Nunn. *Attention Deficit Disorder.* Danbury, Conn.: Franklin Watts, 2001.

Index